God Saves JERUSALEM

The story
of King Hezekiah
and King Sennacherib
(2 Kings 18–19 and 2 Chronicles 32:1–23)
for children

Written by Larry Burgdorf
Illustrated by Steven Petruccio

CONCORDIA PUBLISHING HOUSE · SAINT LOUIS

Back then, they had some funny names—
They didn't call boys Tom or James.
They saw one baby in the crib
And named the kid Sennacherib.

Sennacherib grew up to be
As fierce and warlike as can be.
He raised huge armies so that he
Could conquer any enemy.

He conquered cities by the score,
But always wanted more and more.
In fact, he wanted to be king
Of everyone and everything.

He came then to Jerusalem
And sent a messenger to them.
"Surrender now," the message said;
"Give up or you will all be dead."

He sent a giant army there—
Thousands of soldiers everywhere.
Jerusalem had very few;
There just was nothing they could do.

Jerusalem was then a place
That showed forth God's amazing grace.
The temple of the Lord was there,
A place of worship and of prayer.

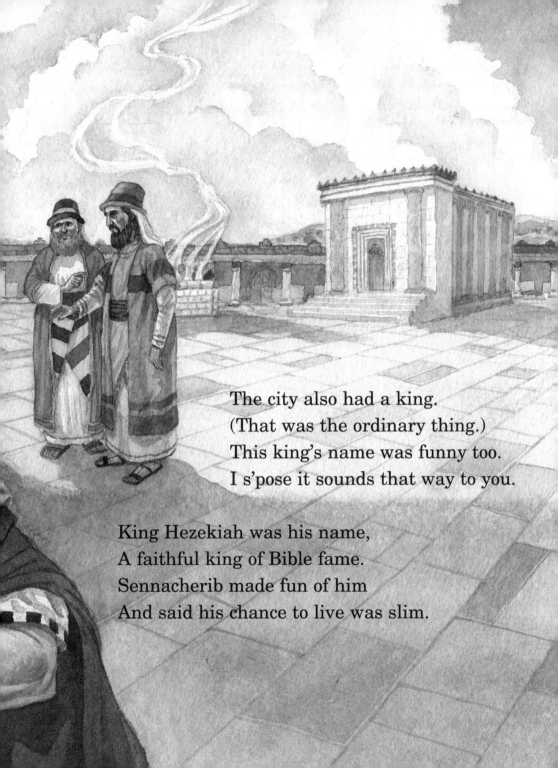

The city also had a king.
(That was the ordinary thing.)
This king's name was funny too.
I s'pose it sounds that way to you.

King Hezekiah was his name,
A faithful king of Bible fame.
Sennacherib made fun of him
And said his chance to live was slim.

He lied to Hezekiah too
And said God told him what to do.
(The god he worshiped was not real.
It couldn't talk or think or feel.)

But then he mocked the true God too.
That was a foolish thing to do.
In fact, it was a huge mistake—
As huge as anyone could make.

King Hezekiah went that day
Into the temple court to pray.
He asked the Lord what he could do
Because his soldiers were so few.

God's word to Hezekiah was
His city would be saved because
The Lord Himself would rescue it
And force Sennacherib to quit.

In spite of Hezekiah's prayer,
That giant army was still there.
Those thousands waited by the hill,
Prepared to slash and burn and kill.

But God sent in His angel then.
That army's days were over when
The angel swept away their breath
And left them cold and still in death.

Jerusalem was saved that day,
And when the angel went away,
The people saw without a doubt
That whole huge army was wiped out.

As God protected that great place,
He shows the least of us His grace.
He sends His angels just for you
To keep you safe in what you do.

And when your life is over here,
There still is nothing you need fear:
Angels will bring you to that place
Where you will see Him face to face.

Dear Parents,

The Bible, in 2 Kings and 2 Chronicles, tells us that King Hezekiah was a man of great faith who brought unity among God's people, restored the practice of Passover worship, and worked to return the temple to its place of glory and rightful use. These accomplishments make him a hero of the Old Testament. Yet the Assyrian king, Sennacherib, was a great ruler in his own right. He had conquered many nations in building up his empire, and he had accumulated vast wealth and power. In his efforts to expand Nineveh, Sennacherib is credited with building the infrastructure that made the hanging gardens of Babylon possible.

When Sennacherib sent his army to conquer Jerusalem, he sent a message with them: the God of Israel was insignificant. Sennacherib's great sin was unbelief, a direct contrast to Hezekiah's unshakable belief in the God of Israel. God answered faithful Hezekiah's prayer and sent an angel to destroy the Assyrian army gathered around Jerusalem—all 185,000 of them, all at the same time.

It's difficult for us to imagine such a battle happening today, but what we can learn from this biblical account is that the Lord God is faithful to His people, hears our prayers, and delivers us from our enemies—sin, death, and the devil—through His Son, Jesus Christ. To Him be the glory!

The Editor